Pokémon Go

The ULTIMATE Guide

Jake Neistat

Introduction

Pokémon is one of the most adored, time-tested, and influential franchises in the entire world. Previously known as Capsule Monsters as well as Pocket Monsters, the Pokémon craze has been going strong and amassing millions of fans for over two decades with no shows signs of slowing down anytime soon. Created by Satoshi Tajiri in 1995, the franchise is centered on a wide variety of fictional creatures of known as Pokémon. Humans, known in this world as Pokémon Trainers, attempt to catch, train, and battle Pokémon with other Pokémon trainers for sport. As a child, Tajiri had a fondness for capturing tadpoles and insects, and decided to take his love for capturing creatures to the next level and successfully pitched the idea to Nintendo executives.

In simple terms, a Pokémon is a small animal-like creature. There are countless different types of Pokémon. The best way for an outsider to the franchise to think about this is different species and breeds of animals. The most well-known Pokémon is without question Pikachu. Even if you're unfamiliar with the Pokémon franchise, you're bound to recognize this cute, electric mouse.

What is Pokémon Go?

You'd be hard pressed to find anyone who isn't aware of Pokémon GO at this point. Most recently, the game overtook Tinder in total users and Twitter in daily users. So, just what is Pokémon GO? Pokémon GO is a free-to-download app that allows users journey outside in an attempt to capture, train, and battle Pokémon. The combination of real world environments and virtually rendered Pokémon provide the user with a unique and exciting augmented reality experience. The ingenious application utilizes your phone's GPS, camera, and clock to detect where you are and makes various Pokémon appear on your screen. As you move, more types of Pokémon will appear depending on your location and time. The idea behind the game is to encourage users to trek around the real world to "catch them all."

You might be asking yourself, "Why in the world is game so popular? Why are people aimlessly wandering around staring at their phones?" The first reason behind the game's popularity is the price. Pokémon GO is available completely free of charge and it's extremely easy to download. Most importantly, fans of the Pokémon franchise are now able to live their fantasies and answer the question they've been asking years, "What if Pokémon were real and existed in our world?"

Currently, the Pokémon GO app is available for iOS and Android in the United States, Australia, and New Zealand. If you're not located in one of those areas, don't get discouraged. The creators of the application, Niantic, have pre-planned releases to other areas as time goes on (Asia and European releases are set to follow soon).

How to play

Getting started

The first step to playing Pokémon GO is downloading the app. Visit your app store and simply search Pokémon GO. The game should populate as the first result and, if you're unsure of whether have the right one, look for Niantic as the developer. The image above is from the iOS app store. Here's a step by step break down of how to download the game:

1. Open the **App Store** from your home screen.
2. **Search** and enter 'Pokémon Go'.
3. Navigate to **Free** tab.
4. **Install** the application.
5. Authorize with **Touch ID** or enter your password.
6. Return to your **home screen**.
7. Tap the **Pokémon Go** icon once the download is complete.
8. On the sign up screen, tap the **Google icon**.
9. Enter your **Google username**. (Alternatively, tap **Create account** and follow instructions).
10. Enter your **Google password**.
11. If applicable, follow **two-factor authentication** procedure.

Once downloaded, open the application and sign up using either your Google account or sign up for a Pokémon Trainer Club account; personally, I've had a better experience using my Google account than signing up for the Pokémon Trainer Club, but either way should work. After signing up, you're given the option to customize your virtual avatar. You can choose the color and style of your avatar's hair, eye color, skin color, shirt, shoes, pants, backpack, as well as your avatar's gender.

Once you're logged in, you'll be greeted by Professor Willow. The Professor provides an introduction to the game and its objective, and walks the player through the process of catching their choice of three "starter Pokémon." You can choose from Charmander, Squirtle, or Bulbasaur; those name will be very familiar to longtime Pokémon fanatics.

After your first Pokémon capture, the game leaves you to own your devices. This can be a bit challenging and confusing, but just keep in mind the game only has three basic parts:

1. Capturing Pokémon
2. Locating and Visiting PokéStops
3. Pokémon Gym Battles

Breakdown of the Main Screen

There's a Pokémon nearby!

The view after capturing your first Pokémon is the main game area and it is essentially a brightly colored animated version of Google Maps. You'll see a geographical breakdown of the surrounding area including houses and buildings, marked and unmarked roads, rustling leaves and grass (which mean a Pokémon is nearby), and local landmarks and points of interest which double as PokéStops and Pokémon Gyms. As you walk, run, or drive about in the real world, your avatar will mirror your movements.

Various Pokémon of all colors, shapes, sizes, and species will pop up on your map as your travel along. If you tap on the Pokémon, you will be able to attempt to capture it in a PokéBall. Here is a detailed breakdown of the main screen icons and their functions:

Player Icon: Your avatar player icon is located in the bottom left corner of the screen. You can tap on the player icon to view information and statistics on your character, including a list of in-game achievements.

PokéBall Icon: The PokéBall Icon in located in the bottom center of the screen. Tapping the **PokéBall** will expand a list of options to choose from:

Items: This is where all of the **Items** you've earned or purchased during your adventure are stored.

Pokédex: This is your personal index of Pokémon. The **Pokédex** will show detailed information on all of the Pokémon species you've previously captured, including the Pokémon's CP (Creature Power).

Pokémon: You can capture the same Pokémon an infinite number of times. Doing so will allow you to upgrade and eventually evolve the Pokémon by earning special candy to feed to the Pokémon. Upgrading and evolving Pokémon can be done from the **Pokémon** icon.

Shop: This is where all of the in-game purchases are made. When playing Pokémon Go, it's extremely easy to run out of PokéBalls while capturing creatures. You can earn additional PokéBalls by visiting PokéStops, or you can purchase them for a small fee. You can also purchase various **Items** at the **Shop**.

Settings and Tips: Located at the top right of the screen within the PokéBall screen, you can quick tips about game strategy as well as adjust in-game settings such as music and sound effect levels as disable vibration, enable the battery saver option, or opt to receive information, offers, promotions, and news updates about Pokémon go via email.

Nearby Pokémon: There is a small rectangle at the bottom right corner of the screen which allows the player to see which Pokémon are close. If you've previously caught the Pokémon, it will appear in full color. If a new Pokémon is nearby, it will appear as a shadowed silhouette in the Nearby Pokémon Screen.

Tracking and Locating Pokémon

Tapping on the aforementioned **Nearby Pokémon** box will present the player with an assortment of up to nine Pokémon that are in the surrounding area. As you and your character walk around the real world and Pokémon world respectively, small purple and gray radar circle emanates from your avatar character. This radar represents the range in which you're able to track surrounding Pokémon.

The "radar ring" also allows you to catch Pokémon without having to walk through treacherous landscapes or enter private property. The radar essentially reaches the Pokémon and brings them out of their hiding spots, allowing you the opportunity to catch them.

There's also a tiny radar box displayed in green that emits from the **Nearby Pokémon** box. Many assume that this radar indicates that you're getting closer to a nearby Pokémon, but, in all actuality, this green radar lets the player know that list of **Nearby Pokémon** is updating. This can mean one of three things:

1. The Pokémon you're approaching is getting closer.
2. The Pokémon you're attempting to capture is getting further away.
3. New Pokémon are populating on the nearby list

It's definitely worth investigating if you notice the green radar emitting from the **Nearby Pokémon** box. The most elusive of all Pokémon could be only a few steps away!

Tracking Evolved and Rare Pokémon

As I previously mentioned, most of your Pokémon are evolved by feeding them special candy. You're also able to capture the evolved version of your Pokémon, as well as extremely rare Pokémon creatures. Rare Pokémon typically hide in very specific places at specific times in the day. If you're goal is to catch a Zubat, Clefairy, or any other nocturnal Pokémon, your best bet is to hunt for them at night. Likewise, you'll find certain Pokémon close to the real-world counterpart of their element (Magikarp or any other water based Pokémon near actual bodies of water).

Evolved Pokémon are much harder to come across than their unevolved Pokémon equivalents, but you'll find them both in the same general areas. The best way to find evolved Pokémon is to constantly check your radar and Nearby Pokémon list.

One thing to keep in mind is rarer Pokémon have higher levels of CP. This also means that the rare Pokémon are much more difficult to capture. High-level Pokémon typically have orange glowing circles around them, as opposed to green with typical Pokémon. The rare, high-level Pokémon can sometimes escape PokéBalls multiple times, so it very well may take several throws before they are truly capture. Once your character has reached a certain Pokémon trainer level, you'll be able to purchase Razz Berries from the shop to feed wild Pokémon. Feeding Razz Berries to Pokémon temporarily weakens them so they're easier to catch, which is extremely beneficial when catching rare or evolved Pokémon.

Capturing Pokémon

The most addictive part of the game is undoubtedly capturing new Pokémon. In order to capture Pokémon, you first have to find them. We already talked about the Nearby Pokémon box, but there are a few aspects you need to be aware of in order to capture them. Each Pokémon has a distance rating in the Nearby Pokémon box, and it's tracked by footprints:

- Zero footprints mean that the Pokémon you're hunting in extremely close and should pop-up at any moment.
- One footprints mean that you're on the right track.
- Two footprints indicate that the Pokémon is a short distance away.
- Three footprints mean that the Pokémon is in the area, but a bit of a distance from your location.

As you get close to the Pokémon, it's distance footprint rating decreases and they are populated into the Nearby Pokémon box. Another way to determine when you're getting close to a Pokémon is the rustling of leaves and grass on your map. Don't get too excited and wander somewhere you're not supposed to be; the rustling merely indicates that a Pokémon is in the general area. Overall, the best indication that you're close enough to capture a Pokémon is that, if enable, your phone will vibrate and the creature will appear on the map. Once the creature

You can also make the Pokémon come out of hiding and come to you or capturing them without walking through various items, tactics, and strategies:

- **Leave the Application Running**: You can plug your phone in and find something else to occupy your time. While this sounds a bit silly, keeping the game up and running dramatically increases your chances of coming across Pokémon.

- **Use an Incense Pot**: You're given incense pots when you first start playing Pokémon GO. You can also earn or buy additional incense pots. Incense essentially draws nearby Pokémon to your general vicinity, so you don't have to hunt as hard to find new creatures. Please following these steps to activate available incense pots:

INCENSE   8 INCENSE   25 INCENSE

◉ 80   ◉ 500   ◉ 1250

- On the main screen, tap the **PokéBall** icon located on the bottom center of the screen.
- Tap **Items**
- Tap **Incense Pot** icon
- The incense pot will then appear on your main screen. You must then tap the pot again to activate it; doing so will lure nearby Pokémon for a total of thirty minutes (the thirty-minute time period continues to countdown even if you close the app, so use the

incense whenever you have thirty minutes to devote to gameplay).

- **Use a Lure**: A lure is essentially a powered-up form of incense and produces better results. You are able to use lures at all PokéStops. Unlike incense which only benefit you as a player, lures benefit all other players at the PokéStop, so it's a quick way to gain allies and new Pokémon friends. Please use the following guide:
  - Locate a PokéStop by tapping it on the map, and then travel to the PokéStop location.
  - You'll be able to determine if there is an active Lure Module by noting if there is pink petals floating around the PokéStop on your map. If not, you should be able to use one of your available lures.
  - Tap the rectangle on the top of the screen that reads "Empty Module slot."
  - Tap one more time to add a Lure Module from your inventory of items.

- **Drive Around**: While this somewhat defeats the idea of getting out and adventuring, this is an easy way (provided you have some way to drive you around) to amass a Pokédex full of new and elusive Pokémon. I've capture plenty of Pokémon which would have been impossible to capture had I not been riding in a car.

Now that a Pokémon has appeared on your screen, it's time to capture the Pokémon! Tap on the Pokémon to zoom into your real world location. This is accomplished by the app using your phone's rear camera, which puts the wild Pokémon right in front of you! You can move your device from left to right to put the Pokémon in frame and to line up your PokéBall for capturing. As I previously mentioned, you're initially given quite a few PokéBalls, but the supplies can quickly dwindle. You can earn additional PokéBalls or purchase them from the in-app Shop.

Depending on the Pokémon you come across, you'll either see a green, orange, or red glowing ring around the Pokémon's avatar. This colored rind indicates the difficulty of capture for the specific Pokémon. A green Pokémon can be capture with very little difficulty; poor and inaccurate throws are sometimes enough to capture the green Pokémon. A red Pokémon requires throwing accuracy and, in some instances, higher-level PokéBalls or treats such as Razz Berries. The following step by step guide walks you through the easiest way to catch a Pokémon in Pokémon GO:

- Make sure the Pokémon you're wanting to capture is in plain view.
- Tap and hold on the PokéBall located in the bottom center of the screen.
- Wait until the green/orange/red rings gets to its smallest size, and then quickly slide your finger toward the Pokémon while releasing your hold on the PokéBall.

- A successful PokéBall through will result in the PokéBall hitting the creature before it disappears into the PokéBall. You can earn extra points if you knock the Pokémon directly on the tip of the head.

You'll have to be able to adjust your PokéBall throws, as different Pokémon require different techniques. Flying Pokémon such as Spearow are a little more difficult to capture within a PokéBall because their onscreen position and distance can change within an instant as they fly about. If you'd like to earn additional catch bonuses and make things interesting, you're able throw a "Curve Ball." Basically, throwing Curve Ball consists of spinning the PokéBall with your fingertip before tossing it and then hitting the Pokémon squarely on top of the creature's head. You must be prepared to lose quite a few PokéBalls while getting the technique down because it can be a bit tricky just starting out. Follow these steps to throw the perfect Curve Ball:

- With the Pokémon in view, tap and hold the PokéBall while starting to spin it in a clockwise or counter-clockwise rotation.
- What until the green/orange/red glowing ring gets to its smallest point, and then flick your finger towards the Pokémon.
- If you do this correctly, you can earn an additional 10XP Curve Ball bonus.

Getting Ready for Battle: Power-Ups and Evolving

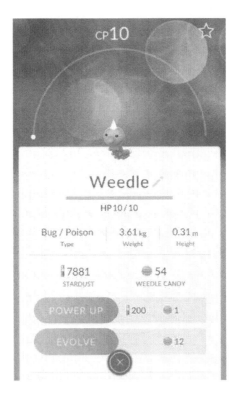

The secret to evolving and increasing the CP of your captured Pokémon is quite simple; you need to capture more Pokémon. The CP allows your Pokémon to grow more valuable in terms of battles against similarly ranked Pokémon at gyms by increasing your Pokémon's hit point and durability effectiveness.

Evolving helps at the gym as well by providing as substantial increase in CP, health, and, in some cases, new abilities for battle. We talked previously about using candy to start a Pokémon's evolution, but we never really dove into how candy is accumulated and how stardust helps your Pokémon as well. Candy and stardust are two in-game items in Pokémon GO that you cannot buy at the store or trade with other Pokémon trainers. Candy and stardust are only found through exploration.

Stardust has the sole purposes of raising your Pokémon's CP, while Pokémon specific candy has two purposes. Candy can be used concurrently with stardust to increase your Pokémon's CP, or it can be used alone to increase evolve your Pokémon. Every specific Pokémon requires a species specific candy, while stardust is universal and can be used towards any captured Pokémon. Each Pokémon requires a specific number of candy in order to evolve.

With all this talk about candy and stardust, you're probably wondering where exactly to get these items. Anytime your capture a Pokémon after your trainer level is increase, you'll earn stardust (your training level is increased by capturing Pokémon, throwing accurately, gym battles, etc.).

Breed specific candy is obtained once after catching a Pokémon. You typically earn five to ten pieces the first time you capture a specific breed, and then three to five piece of candy once you capture the same breed again. You also have the option transferring an extra version of a capture Pokémon to Professor Willow, which will earn you one piece of candy. So even if you already have a certain Pokémon, it's important to continue capturing the duplicate versions. When I first started playing, I didn't truly understand the importance of capturing the same Pokémon, and passed up so many Rattata and Pidgy duplicates.

To actually level up and increase your Pokémon's CP, you'll need one piece of candy and 200-800 bits of Stardust on average. This will result in a 20-80 point CP increase for your Pokémon. You can also evolve your Pokémon just by using your accumulated candy pieces. Most Pokémon take approximately 10 pieces of candy, but it takes a lot more to evolve certain types of Pokémon (to evolve Magikarp into Gyarados, it takes 800 pieces of candy). To level up or evolve your Pokémon, please follow these steps:

- While on the main screen, tap the PokéBall in the bottom center of the screen.
- Tap on the Pokémon button.
- Select the Pokémon you want to level up or evolve.
- Towards the bottom of this screen, there are options labeled Power Up and Evolve. Select what you like to do give you have enough items to do so; the cost

of each action is listed on the right, with your total count of stardust/candy listed above.

If you find yourself unable to evolve or power up a Pokémon and you have the correct amount of stardust and/or candy, it's more than likely that your Pokémon trainer level is too low. Controlling a Pokémon with an elevated CP level isn't possible with a low Pokémon trainer level, so you'll need to increase this first (again by capturing more Pokémon and winning more Pokémon Gym battles to increase your trainer XP).

Gym Battle Success

Before thinking about traveling to a gym and battling other Pokémon, you must first reach level five as a Pokémon trainer. Once you reach that point, a whole new Pokémon world is at your fingertips. You're now able to journey to gyms and battle your friends, foes, and complete strangers.

The gyms are surprisingly easy to find via the Pokémon GO map. They are the buildings on the animated map that are the tallest are and largest, and are represented in the real world by landmarks or buildings. You aren't able to actually battle at the gym unless you're in the general vicinity of the real-world gym counterpart.

Teams

The first thing you're asked to do once reach a gym is choose a Pokémon team. You have the option of joining the Instinct (Yellow) team, Mystic (Blue) team, or the Valor (Red) team. When you participate in gym battles, you're doing so to gain or preserve your team's control of said gym. Now you just have to decide what team to join. Contrary to popular belief, your chosen team isn't necessarily that important; the gameplay is the same no matter your team and one team isn't fundamentally better than the other. What ultimately matters is how well your team works as a cohesive unit. Here's a breakdown of the teams and their features if you need helping with your decision:

- **Team Instinct** (Yellow): **Team Instinct** is led by Spark, and the philosophy of this team is trusting your gut and following your instincts. If you believe that winning battles are a matter of trusting your intuition, this is the team for you. The mascot for **Team Instinct** is the legendary flying Pokémon, Zapdos.

- **Team Mystic** (Blue): **Team Mystic** is led by Blanche, and this team operates by means of strategic analysis and rational thought; **Team Mystic** almost has a scientific approach to Pokémon gym battles. The mascot for **Team Mystic** is the legendary icy bid, Articuno.

- **Team Valor** (Red): Team Valor is led by Candela, and this team focuses on strength and training. If you believe the most important thing is to establish a bond with your Pokémon through intense training regiments and power-ups, this is the team for you. Team Valor is represented by Moltres.

According to the most recent statistics, Team Mystic has the most members. Team Valor comes in second in terms of member count, leaving Team Instinct with the fewest members thus far. One thing to keep in mind is that you cannot change your team once you've selected one, so you might want to ask friends who play Pokémon GO about their affiliation before making your selection.

Training

At this point in Pokémon GO's lifecycle, all the gyms have been claimed by a team, so you'll be unable to simply walk up and claim one. I would not recommend wasting any time battling Pokémon that you simply cannot beat. If you're Pokémon has a lower CP rating, you'll more than likely lose that fight. The best way to train your Pokémon for battle is to go to a gym already controlled by your team and compete in friendly battles against fellow teammates. This will help you learn the ins and outs of battling, as well as earn you additional trainer XP.

Additionally, these friendly battles also serve as protection against rival teams and gyms. Your team can earn "Prestige" from engaging in friendly battles, and this is how many gyms get to be at such as high level. Essentially, if your team owns a gym you're battling at, you can choose a single Pokémon to fight to raise the gym's overall Prestige points. Prestige points determine how many Pokémon can be stationed at a single gym. The more Pokémon that are stationed at a gym, the harder that gym is to capture and control by rival teams. You also collect higher bonuses for having more Pokémon at a single gym. Since we're on the topic of Gym strength, let's dive right into the topic of Gym Levels.

Gym Levels

Gym Levels basically indicate how many Pokémon you can expect to battle before controlling said gym. If the Gym Level is at a level 1, you will have to fight and defeat one Pokémon to potentially take the gym over. If the Gym Level is at level 2, you will have to engage and defeat two Pokémon before having a chance to take the gym over. You're able to determine the Pokémon and their CP that you have to battle (and in which order you will battle them) by swiping through the Pokémon listed for the gym in question.

Type Advantages

This is an aspect of the game that's overlooked by many players.   Longtime fans of the Pokémon franchise know that each specific Pokémon has a type or multiple types. Essentially, a Pokémon's typing will help you determine its strengths and weaknesses in regards to battling.   Just as with previous games, the Pokémon typing play a huge role in gym battles in Pokémon GO, especially when deciding what team or gym to challenge.

When you're set to battle against a rival team's Gym, you're allowed to take along six of your Pokémon; will touch more on the battle roster later on. If you already know what Pokémon you'll be battling against, it's best to plan ahead (the first trainer you'll battle will be above the gym location on your map). For example, you may come across a gym that has a Pinsiras as the first Pokémon to battle. Pinsir is a Bug-type Pokémon and Bug-types are vulnerable against Flying, Rock, and Fire type attacks.

39

Having this knowledge will allow you to take Pokémon in your arsenal that possess those kind of attacks. Attacking a Pokémon's vulnerabilities inflict far more damage than typical attacks.

Resistance is also something to consider choosing your battle team. From our previous example, we know that Pinsir is a Bug-type Pokémon and thusly has Bug-type attacks in its repertoire. Fire, Flying, Poison, Fighting, Fairy, and Steel type Pokémon are all extremely resistant to Bug-type attacks, so Pinsir would be virtually useless against these type of Pokémon. While you can't prepare for everything, knowing and comprehending Pokémon type advantages and disadvantages will tremendously increase your chances of victory in gym battles.

Move-sets

While looking at the statistics of your captured Pokémon, you might notice that each one has two unique moves; standard attack and special move. To execute a standard attack, you simple tap on the opposing Pokémon you're battling. To launch a special attack, it takes much more energy and a little more time. You'll need to tap and hold your own Pokémon to launch the special move; special moves are naturally stronger and more damaging than standard attacks, and the special moves vary by Pokémon.

In order to use the special move, you'll need to first build up the adequate amount of energy. To build energy while battling, you'll need to dodge your opponent's attacks by swiping left or right and perform standard/fast attacks. Here is a comprehensive list of standard attacks, as well as special attacks, to help with your planning and strategy:

Standard Attack Name	Attack Type	Damage Rating
Acid	Poison	10
Bit	Dark	6
Bubble	Water	15
Bug Bite	Bug	6
Bullet Punch	Steel	10
Confusion	Psychic	12
Dragon Breath	Dragon	6
Ember	Fire	10
Feint Attack	Dark	12
Fire Fang	Fire	7
Frost Breath	Ice	12
Fury Cuter	Bug	3
Ice Shard	Ice	10
Karate Chop	Fight	6
Lick	Ghost	10
Low Kick	Fight	5
Metal Claw	Steel	12
Mud Shot	Ground	12
Mud Slap	Ground	6
Peck	Flying	10
Poison Jab	Poison	15
Poison Sting	Poison	6
Pound	Normal	8
Psycho Cut	Psychic	15
Quick Attack	Normal	10
Razor Leaf	Grass	15
Rock Smash	Fight	5
Rock Throw	Rock	12
Scratch	Normal	10
Shadow Claw	Ghost	16
Spark	Electric	7
Splash	Water	0
Steel Wing	Steel	15
Tackle	Normal	12
Thunder Shock	Electric	5
Vine Whip	Grass	10

Water Gun	Water	10
Wing Attack	Flying	12
Zen Headbutt	Psychic	15

Special Attack Name	Attack Type	Damage Rating
Aerial Ace	Flying	25
Air Cutter	Flying	25
Ancient Power	Rock	30
Aqua Jet	Water	15
Blizzard	Ice	60
Body Slam	Normal	50
Bone Club	Ground	20
Brick Break	Fight	30
Brine	Water	15
Bubble Beam	Water	25
Bulldoze	Ground	30
Cross Chop	Fight	55
Cross Poison	Poison	20
Dark Pulse	Dark	45
Dazzling Gleam	Fairy	45
Dig	Ground	45
Disarming Voice	Fairy	20
Discharge	Electric	40
Dragon Claw	Dragon	40
Dragon Pulse	Dragon	50
Draining Kiss	Fairy	15
Drill Peck	Flying	30
Drill Run	Ground	30
Earthquake	Ground	60
Fire Blast	Fire	60
Fire Punch	Fire	35
Flame Burst	Fire	25
Flame Charge	Fire	25
Flame Wheel	Fire	35
Flamethrower	Fire	50
Flash Cannon	Steel	55
Gunk Shot	Poison	60
Horn Attack	Normal	20
Hurricane	Flying	60
Hydro Pump	Water	60
Hyper Beam	Normal	70

Hyper Fang	Normal	35
Ice Beam	Ice	50
Icy Wind	Ice	15
Iron Head	Steel	40
Leaf Blade	Grass	45
Low Sweep	Fight	25
Magnet Bomb	Steel	25
Megahorn	Bug	55
Moonblast	Fairy	60
Mud Bomb	Ground	25
Night Slash	Dark	25
Ominous Wind	Ghost	25
Petal Blizzard	Grass	50
Play Rough	Fairy	50
Poison Fang	Poison	15
Power Gem	Rock	40
Power Whip	Grass	60
Psybeam	Psychic	35
Psychic	Psychic	50
Psyschock	Psychic	40
Rock Slide	Rock	40
Scald	Water	35
Seed Bomb	Grass	30
Shadow Ball	Ghost	40
Signal Beam	Big	35
Sludge	Poison	25
Sludge Wave	Poison	60
Solar Beam	Grass	65
Stomp	Normal	25
Stone Edge	Rock	55
Struggle	Normal	15
Submission	Fight	30
Swift	Normal	25
Thunder	Electric	65
Thunder Punch	Electric	40
Thunderbolt	Electric	50
Twister	Dragon	15
Vice Grip	Normal	15

Water Pulse	Water	30
Wrap	Normal	15
X-Scissor	Bug	30

Another aspect you need to consider with a Pokémon's move-set is that Pokémon's evolution. If you catch a Pokémon that does not evolve, that Pokémon's move-set will not change. However, Pokémon that can evolve can experience attack changes. According to some players, every Pokémon can have one of two standard attack moves, and one of three special attack moves. Unfortunately, there currently isn't a perfect formula to determine what moves will change when you evolve a Pokémon, so it can be challenging to achieve the desired move-set.

Multiple Pokémon

We briefly touched base on the importance of gathering duplicate Pokémon in terms of gaining Power-Ups, Evolving, and Transferring duplicates to Professor Willow, but we didn't touch base on how duplicates can be beneficial in terms of move-sets and attacks. Duplicate Pokémon of the same species can actually have different move-sets. For example, a player can have a Pidgey Pokémon with two drastically different move-sets:

- The first Pidgey could have a Quick Attack for its standard move and the Air Cutter Attack for its special move
- The second Pidgey could have a Tackle Attack for its standard move and Twister Attack for its special move. If you refer to the breakdown of move-types above, you'll notice that a Twister is a Dragon-type attack, which can be extremely effective if you're looking to defeat a Dragon-type Pokémon.

There are a lot of advantages and disadvantages to taking two Pokémon of the same species into battle. It will definitely take some trial and error to determine the right assortment of Pokémon for you to take into battle.

Battling

Pokémon GO auto-populates your roster of six Pokémon for gym battles, but that doesn't mean those are the six creatures. You can change the Pokémon in your roster and/or you can change their entry order simply by tapping on any of the Pokémon in your roster and swapping their position or swapping them out for another Pokémon before entering a battle. Logically, you'll want you most powerful Pokémon (in regards to CP levels) on your roster.

Battling is actually quite simple. Just like when you first started throwing PokéBalls to capture Pokémon, the controls are simplistic but can take some getting used to. To battle other trainers' Pokémon, you'll only need to learn three easy commands: Tap, swipe, and hold. We touched on this earlier, but here is a more detailed breakdown of how you apply each battle command:

- Standard/Fast Attack: To perform a standard attack, tap your Pokémon to perform a standard attack.
- Dodging: To dodge an attack, swipe left or right in to opposite direction of the opposing Pokémon's attacks.
- Special Attack: To perform your Pokémon's special attack, you must first make sure your special attack meter is fully charged; you can charge this meter by dodging attacks and by successfully utilizing standard attacks. Once your meter is full,

tap and hold your Pokémon. This will engage your special attack and will potentially cause large amounts of damage for the opposition's Pokémon.

Healing Defeated Pokémon

More than likely, you're going to lose your first Pokémon Gym Battle. You will eventually lose a battle, even if you win your first; you can certainly catch them all, but you can't win them all. There seems to be some misconception that if you lose a gym battle, you lose your Pokémon. Just because you lose a battle doesn't mean your Pokémon is gone forever. Although weakened after a lost battle, Pokémon can be healed and revived by using various Revive and Portion items.

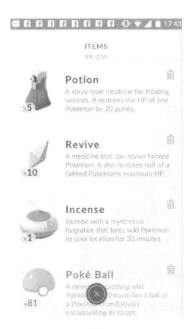

After a lost battle, follow the steps below to heal your defeated Pokémon:

- Tap the PokéBall in the bottom center of the screen.
- Select the Items icon.
- The game should then load a screen showing you the Pokémon you've captured that need the items in your collection. I find it's easiest to organize my Pokémon by CP, which allows you to quickly and easily determine which Pokémon to heal and maximize strengths.

Although Pokémon GO isn't the most intuitive or easiest game on the market, it's extremely fun and rewarding! If you want to be a Pokémon Master, you'll need to put in the time and effort. Practice makes perfect is an age old saying, and it holds true in the case of Pokémon GO. The more you play, the better you'll become.

Tips, Tricks and Secrets of Pokémon GO

Here are some tricks, tips, and little-known secrets to help you get the most of Pokémon GO and enjoy it as much as possible.

Hatching Eggs

More than likely, you've gathered some eggs at this point. Eggs are hidden all throughout the game (some have even been found in the submenu after clicking on the PokéBall). Once you gather some eggs, you will place them in the egg incubator. For the eggs to hatch, you must walk a certain amount of steps (some eggs take two kilometers of steps before hatching, while others take ten kilometers). One would assume you can simple go for a car ride to hatch the eggs, but Pokémon GO can detect these cheating tactics. You need to cover the designated KM distance at a relatively low rate of speed. Many individuals have combatted this and cheated the system through bike riding, while others have simply attached their device to a ceiling fan and turned the fan on at the lowest speed. Both methods seem to be effective with hatching incubated eggs. Most recently, I heard a tale of a player successfully hatching eggs by taping their device to the top of their Roomba.

Hearing Pokémon

After capturing a Pokémon, you can hear what sound that Pokémon makes. Who doesn't want to hear what their Pokémon sounds like? You'll simply need to tap the PokéBall at the bottom center of the screen and then access the Pokémon submenu. From there, select the Pokémon you'd like to hear. When that Pokémon's character screen opens, make sure your device's volume it turned up and tap on the Pokémon image to hear that creature's scream.

Using Incense and Lucky Egg Simultaneously

If you happen to come across a Lucky Egg, it will allow you to earn double XP for a time period of 30 minutes. An easy way to earn XP points are by capturing and/or evolving Pokémon (catching a new Pokémon will earn you 100XP, while evolving Pokémon will earn you 500XP). When you utilize a Lucky Egg, you'll earn 200XP for any new Pokémon captures, and you'll earn 1,000 XP for any Pokémon you evolve (which is why many players wait to evolve Pokémon until they find a Lucky Egg). If you use an Incense of Lure item simultaneously with a Lucky Egg, you'll have a much greater chance of earning XP points. Lures and Incense attract Pokémon for a 30-minute time period, which is conveniently the same amount of time a Lucky Egg can be used.

Turn off AR for Accuracy

One of the biggest reasons behind the sudden popularity of Pokémon GO is the augmented reality. It's almost surreal to see an actual Pokémon in the real-world. While it certainly is fun to see a wild Pokémon on your front porch, the game's augmented reality feature does cause the Pokémon to shake and jolt around a bit while they synchronize with your camera. You're actually able to turn off the augmented reality function in the game's settings, which will allow you to throw more accurately and increase your catch rates. Once a Pokémon comes into view on your map and you click the Pokémon to allow it to enter our world, you'll see a button at the top right corner labeled "AR." You can turn off the augmented reality there. You won't see the Pokémon on your street, but catching them is much easier.

Wait for the PokéStop to Refresh

PokéStops provide players with extra PokéBalls, eggs, and Pokémon revive items. You can visit a PokéStop, gather up some items and then wait. Many players assume that PokéStops are a once-per-day activity, but the reality is quite the contrary. PokéStops refresh approximately every 5 minutes, so you're able to hang out at a PokéStop and continuously gain new items. Some PokéStops give out rare items (such as the aforementioned Lucky Eggs), so patience is a virtue.

Look for Landmarks

PokéStops are created based off of real world points of interest. If that point of interest holds great significance (such as a local landmark), the Pokéstop will have much better items. If you're on the hunt for rare items, be on the lookout for your town's landmarks.

Start with Pikachu

When you first begin your Pokémon GO journey, you're given the option of one of three starter Pokémon: Squirtle, Charmander, or Bulbasaur. What most people don't realize is that you don't actually have to pick one of those three. Simple ignore the three starter pack Pokémon and begin walking away. Eventually, they will respawn and you'll need to repeat the process (ignore and walk away). If you keep doing this, you'll the Pokémon will respawn with Pikachu in the lineup. You can then select Pikachu as your starter Pokémon.

Pikachu

Don't Stop after Winning a Gym

As I previously mentioned, once you reach level 5, you're able to begin participating in gym battles. This is when the real excitement begins. If you defeated a rival team and took over a gym, don't stop! You'll need to leave Pokémon behind to defend the gym in your absence. Defending a gym for a long period of time will generate coin bonuses which can be collected in the top right section of the shop menu.

Save Data with Offline Maps

Pokémon Go uses map data pulled directly from Google Maps. If you download your home and work areas on your phone via the Google Maps application, it will greatly improve your performance in Pokémon GO. Many have complained about their device constantly having to redraw surrounding and catch up; this seems to solve that issue. You simply need to open Google Maps, select Settings, and then tap "Offline Areas." Next, tap the '+' icon and use the map to draw a squared around the area you want to download. Once your area is mapped out, simply tap "Download." This will help in preserving your mobile data allowance, and it can also improve the battery life of your device.

The most important tip I can give you about Pokémon GO is to get out there and enjoy yourself! Look at Pokémon GO not as a challenge to be conquered, but as a fun escape from the everyday world. Playing Pokémon GO with friends and family is a great way to bond, collaborate, and have a blast. Pokémon GO is about nostalgia, bringing in new fans and, most importantly, it's about having fun. What are you waiting for? Get out there and Catch Em' All!